Survivors in the Frozen North

Story by Beverley Randell
Illustrations by Julian Bruère

Chapter One

Three Months Old

Far away, in the north of the world, Kamit the polar bear cub poked his nose out of a tunnel in the snow. The tunnel led to the cramped winter den where he had been born three months ago.

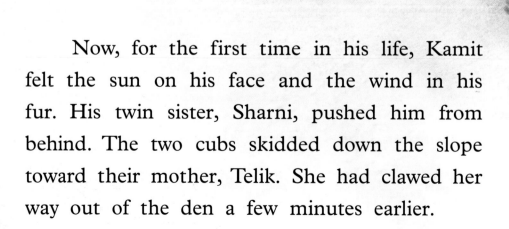

Now, for the first time in his life, Kamit felt the sun on his face and the wind in his fur. His twin sister, Sharni, pushed him from behind. The two cubs skidded down the slope toward their mother, Telik. She had clawed her way out of the den a few minutes earlier.

For a while, the cubs enjoyed tumbling about in the snow. But soon they were tired out, and their mother led them back to the shelter of the den, where she fed them.

Telik was very thin. She had eaten nothing for five whole months! If she did not find food soon, all three of them would die.

A day or two later, Telik decided that her cubs were strong enough to walk to the frozen sea. There she would hunt for seals.

But Kamit and Sharni had short legs, and it was difficult for them to cross the icy ridges. Although Telik was starving, she had to keep stopping to let her tired cubs feed and rest. Her body sheltered them from the freezing wind.

After walking for several days, Telik stopped and lifted her nose in the air. She could smell seals! At last, she had reached the hunting grounds.

Telik soon made her first kill. Now she would not starve to death, and she would be able to go on feeding her cubs.

Down by the frozen sea, Kamit and Sharni were well fed, but the world was still full of danger.

One day, as they walked along, Telik saw a large male bear approaching. She knew that he might try to attack her cubs and eat them!

Telik was smaller than the male bear, but she growled so fiercely that he decided not to risk a fight. He turned back and left the cubs alone.

This time the twins had survived, but Telik was still nervous. She took no chances and hurried them away.

Chapter Two

Six Months Old

Three months later, the cubs were still too small to hunt for their own food. Every day, they followed Telik and learned her skills.

Sometimes she would sit beside a seal's breathing hole, waiting for the seal to come back from catching fish beneath the ice. When the seal put its head above the water to take a breath, Telik would swipe at it with her huge paw. But the seals were quick and wary, and would often escape. Then she would have to try again.

Kamit and Sharni loved to have play-fights. Once, as Telik was waiting silently by a breathing hole, the cubs scuffled with each other. The seal heard them, saw their moving shadows, and was scared away. Telik was angry, and she turned around and cuffed Kamit and Sharni with her large paw.

After that lesson, the cubs knew that they must keep quiet and still while their mother was hunting.

Late in the summer, the thick sea ice began to melt.

One day, Telik crossed some open water between floating islands of ice. Kamit and Sharni, whose paws were smaller, paddled along slowly behind her. They were enjoying their first real swim.

But not for long … A pod of fierce killer whales saw them, and chased them! Telik knew that she had to reach the safety of a large ice floe, but she couldn't leave her cubs behind. In a great hurry, she got Kamit to climb onto her back. Then, with Sharni clinging to her fur, Telik swam for her life!

Telik and her cubs scrambled out of the water just in time! Then they raced away from the edge of the ice, well out of reach of the leaping whales. Telik had saved her cubs from terrible danger, once again.

11

Chapter Three

Two Years Old

Telik took care of her cubs for more than two years. During all that time, she fed them and sheltered them, and protected them from danger. Kamit and Sharni grew to be nearly as big as their mother, but they did not want to leave her. They knew that she would allow them to share all the food that she caught!

But one morning, Telik left her cubs, because she knew that they were big enough to hunt for their own food. She had taught them well, and all that they needed was practice.

At first the cubs wandered about, expecting Telik to come back, but a day later she still had not returned. The twins were now on their own. They felt lonely and hungry.

As the weeks went by, they grew even hungrier. A dead seabird was the only thing they found to eat. They tried to catch seals at their breathing holes, but the seals were too quick for them. Telik had shown her cubs how to hunt, but they were finding it very difficult. They were getting desperate!

Kamit and Sharni could not survive much longer without food.

At last, Kamit saw a seal resting on the ice, with its back to the water. Now he had a chance! He would sneak up behind it.

Kamit lowered himself into the sea, without making a noisy splash. With great care, he swam toward the seal until he was very close to it. He sprang out of the water and killed the seal before it had time to escape.

Sharni hurried to join Kamit, and together they shared a good meal for the first time since their mother had left.

And a few days later, all by herself, Sharni managed to catch a seal at its breathing hole. She shared it with her brother.

Kamit and Sharni had finally learned to take care of themselves. Now they could survive alone in the dangerous frozen world.